# THE COMPETITIVE EDGE:

## How to win after the game is over

A NOVEL BY
TRAVIS LEWIS

Copyright © 2020 Travis Lewis

All rights reserved.

ISBN: 978-1-7330634-8-7

# **DEDICATION**

This book is dedicated to my son Ramsey. Many of these words are meant for you to hear when my voice doesn't have sound anymore. I love you.

# TABLE OF CONTENTS

## ACKNOWLEDGMENTS

## INTRODUCTION

## CHAPTER 1

Attitude for Aptitude: what is attitude and aptitude? How does one affect the other?

## CHAPTER 2

On the Edge: identify where you are and what can be done to move forward

## CHAPTER 3

The Decision Why: what is the decision-making process and why is it so important?

## CHAPTER 4

Self-Image : the importance of self-image and how it relates to being successful

## CHAPTER 5

Failing vs. Quitting: there is a difference between the two and how they relate to success

## CHAPTER 6

Winning and Influencing People: a process of how to win people over by getting them involved and celebrating their success

## CHAPTER 7

Think Big, Act Big, Get Big: success starts in the mind and plays out in the real world. How does that process work?

## CHAPTER 8

Don't Work Me Hard: how does hard work relate to success?

## CHAPTER 9

Momentum and Motivation: how momentum leads to motivation and motivation leads to success

## CHAPTER 10

Being Extraordinary: what is the difference between ordinary and extraordinary?

## ABOUT THE AUTHOR

# ACKNOWLEDGMENTS

I have to say that I was truly blessed and highly favored with the way my life has been up to this point. Things have not been perfect by any means, but everything that I have gone through prepared me for what came next. Learning from failures is truly a part of growth in life. Everything that an African American kid needed to make it, I had. I had a family that loved me. That is all it really takes. All the other obstacles are there to overcome, anyway.

"How to Win After the Game Is Over" is not just about sports, it's about transition. Transition comes in many forms. Coming off the playing field is only one. Losing a job, retiring, or having to move on from a relationship are all types of transition. It's about getting up after you have fallen down. It's about keeping on with the keep-on after what you thought was going to last forever ends. What do you do with all of that passion and drive you had? Do you just let it go to waste?

My mom was 27 with 3 kids to raise on her own after she was told by one man that she wasn't ever going to be anything and abused by another. She won after many others thought the game was over for her. My oldest brother used to get up, drive the bus to school in the morning, go to practice, and then go to work at BI-LO at night when he was still in high school. Still to this day, I've never seen a man do so much for others without asking for anything in return. He was just wired that way.

And to my brother Tre, I can honestly say that he is just one of a kind. He is one of the most clever, strategic human beings I know. As a kid I never saw someone so talented. He was the best basketball player and one of the fastest humans I've seen run as well. If circumstances would have been different I believe he would have been a professional athlete on some level. But that is what this book is all about. What do you do when circumstances don't go your way? I can say that I've seen my brother fall more times than I can count, but when the dust cleared I saw him standing again. That's what the competitive edge is. That's what allows us to win after we think the game is over.

# **INTRODUCTION**

In the spring of 2001, I was going into my senior year of college football. I had worked so hard to get to that point in my life. Coming up in a single-family home in a small town I can't say that there were many great examples outside of my family that projected success. After earning a scholarship to ETSU in 1997 and experiencing some success there I stepped out on faith and pursued my dream of playing major college football. I walked on to the University of South Carolina in the fall of 1999. I had to pay my way this time. I was determined to make it against all odds. I got a job as a server and took a full course load while I was still on the football team. No scholarship, so I HAD to work to pay my rent, car insurance, buy food, and clothes. As I look back at it all I have no idea how I did it, but I knew it had to be done to chase my dreams, so I made it happen. As a transfer I had to sit out that year and could only practice. And practice I did! Every practice was like a game to me. I gave it everything I had to help the guys playing to get better. At the end of that season I was back on full scholarship. The following season We won our 1st bowl game In more than a decade. When spring 2001 rolled around I was ready for my last year of college football. My dream fell apart right in front of my face. The head coach at the university called me into his office and said he was not going to honor my scholarship for the up and coming season, and he was dismissing me from the team. I told him that I did not care about the scholarship money and I just wanted to play ball. He said no and that I would only be a distraction to the team if that were the case. I asked him why he was doing this to me? His response was he saw my grades were slipping and joining a fraternity showed him that I didn't care about my teammates. I was all Academic SEC student and the universities representative for the SEC good works team for outstanding community service and he was telling me this.

At that time, it was the most painful experience of loss I have ever had in my life. Someone else had taken my dreams away from me in one conversation. What he did not do was take away my competitive edge. The game on the field ended but the game of life continued. I could not allow myself to just be defined by what I was on the football field. I was more than that.

I became the first in my family to graduate from a university and went on to become an entrepreneur/ business owner while helping 1000's of others find their paths along the way. The Competitive Edge is in you! It is there! This book will help you to find that Competitive Edge and allow it to guide you where you want to be.

# CHAPTER 1
# Attitude for Aptitude: *what is attitude and aptitude? How does one affect the other?*

If you have ever played a sport, you know what it is like to have a competitive edge, desire to win, be successful, or receive praise for something you have done correctly.

Life is no different. Interestingly enough I've found that there are so many of us out there who are former athletes or people in transition who don't take that competitive edge, that we had in one area of life, and transfer it directly to our success in other areas of life. That is what this is all about. How to transfer that competitive edge into being successful in life and the attitude you must have to do so.

The best place for me to start is at the beginning. How

many of us remember the first sport that we played? Mine was baseball. Back where I am from, we didn't have a little league football team where kids were playing at 7 or 8 years old, so the first thing we could play was T-ball. That is when I learned about my competitive edge as an athlete. I wanted to win, period! I wanted to hit a homerun every single time I went up to bat. If I did not, I was mad. If my teammates did not do well and we lost a game, I was mad at them. Those were things that I had to learn in life were not good for me.

As I got older I began to play fast pitch baseball. I was one of the better baseball players in the league. Being that it was just a little league in a small town, that was not saying much, but for the competition I was still one of the better players. I can remember the last year I played. I led the league in homeruns and ended up being intentionally walked every game. You would think that being a star offensive player, I would make the all-star team. Well, I did not. Why? Because I had a bad attitude. I can remember seeing the all-star selections and not being one of them. I was so angry and upset I walked off the field. That was the last time I played baseball until I got into High school. By that time, other people's skills had caught up with mine. My skills had diminished, and I was not the same player, but could have been had I stuck with the sport. The moral to this story is to not let a negative attitude control the outcomes in your life. You never know how good you can be at something if you keep pursuing it with a positive attitude.

I can tell you for sure that if you stop you will never be as good as you could have been. That is a lesson I had to learn. A lot of people play baseball and they make an exceptionally good living doing so. I took myself away from that opportunity because I had a negative attitude. You have to have a positive attitude in the things that you do whether you are on or off the field.

I once had a job as a cook in a restaurant downtown Charleston, SC. It was a small kitchen. Usually a one-man kitchen, so responsibility to get things done when an order came in fell solely on the cook that was on shift at that particular time. That cook would also be responsible for all the prep work that was left and needed to be done. Nothing strange or uncommon about that scenario at all. When I started in the kitchen I noticed that even though the kitchen was small there was always something that was not getting done that would slow down or stop the flow of work in the kitchen. This led to tons of pointless complaining amongst the kitchen staff. That led to longer ticket times as well as a decline in the quality of the dishes that were being prepared. This was becoming an issue that was noticeable by management and ownership. There had to be a solution to this, but no one could put a finger on what the issue was. What it came down to, was the attitude that: "no one else is doing what was supposed to be done and leaving me to do it." I mean every member of the kitchen would say that! If everyone is saying that, then how is any work getting done? It is not. It had been there no more than 2 months and I was asked to take over the kitchen. It was not something that I wanted to do but it was something that was needed at the time, so I agreed to it short term until I got my own business off the ground again. Things were not smooth. I mean here it is that the newest member of the kitchen staff was put in charge of a whole kitchen that had been there for at least 6-12 months longer than me. Why would management do that? The answer is in the title of this chapter. Attitude! I was not the person to complain about what was. I focused on what is and what does it take to get to where we want. The first thing I made sure of was that I became an example of what I wanted to see in a worker in the kitchen. I did not focus on the physical how to but more on the mental how to. What I mean by that is how to mentally carry the physical load that is coming. Attitude is the sole determining factor of the outcome of the situation. Working with a positive attitude and a positive outlook always yields better results than working with a negative attitude and a negative outlook on things. My favorite quote would be "if you get lemons the best thing you could do is make lemonade!" The lemon may be the situation you face but the sugar is the positive attitude that you carry! The water is a combination of all the things that need to be done to improve the situation. When you get a lemon in life always have your sugar ready to go because there is gonna be some water somewhere around. You can mix the lemon with the water all day but the only way you gonna make it taste sweet is with that sugar! The more the sugar (the more positive the attitude) the better the lemonade taste! As for the kitchen well, things were streamlined while I was there. We lost a few and hired a few more. When I left the kitchen to pursue my own business it was left in the hands of someone I hired while running the kitchen. I can only hope that she followed the same blueprint to get the positive results she wants.

**"Don't let a negative attitude control the outcomes in your life. You never know how good you can be at something if you keep pursuing it with a positive attitude"**

If you have any aspirations of being a boss and having your own your attitude is going to be a direct reflection of how far you go. I can assure you that if you ever want to be the leader of an organization you better have an attitude that you are prepared to be the last person standing even if no one else is. I remember going to a leadership conference in 2007 and listening to one of the company's executives talk about attitude and mentality. I was a bit frustrated and confused at the time because the person that mentored me in this particular business had decided to leave the company.

I remembered not wanting to trust anyone! Especially the guys that trained him. I never got a positive or sincere vibe from those guys, so I never got close to them. I still allowed myself to take in the information that was being passed along. One of them made a comment that has stuck with me since I heard it. It is an attitude and mentality a person has to have when looking at the face of adversity. He said, "Be the last person standing and you will stand next to me." That is an attitude and a mentality I will talk more about in chapter 5 "Failing vs. Quitting"

# Chapter 2
# On The Edge:

### Identify where you are and what can be done to move forward

As we go through life we are all going to get to that point where we have to decide to stay on the platform we are on or jump to chase other opportunities. I'm going to break it down so we can get an understanding of how it works. We are all on a platform, and there is an edge to that platform of life that we are all on. The platform is a representation of where we are in life and how far we have come from where we started. The edge is a representation of that next step beyond where we see ourselves on that platform. For some of us, we get to that edge, which is a median for comfort in our lives, and we never go past that point. Some of us survive and do fairly well in life, while others may struggle. Regardless of where we are on the platform we are on, once we get to that edge we stay or go. We have a decision to stay where we are or continue to move forward.

There are 3 types of people out there. You have wishers, watchers, and makers. Some people sit on their platform and dream about what it is like to get to that edge and take that jump. They imagine it in their minds and that is the extent of action for those people. They are wishers. There are some people who will look "out there" past the edge and see all of the things they want to have and do in their lives, and they will see other people out there doing and living those things. Those people are called watchers. They watch other people make it happen and that is the extent of their action. The next group of people are the ones that have gone to the edge and beyond, living their dreams. They are the makers. They actually follow through with taking what was created in the mind and doing the work that it takes to give it life.

Then comes the question: What did those people, who are out there living their dreams, do once they got to that same ledge? If you ask them they will all say the same thing: THEY JUMPED! Sometimes when you are looking at those people that are out there living their lives you will find yourself looking down off of that edge and you will see people at the bottom of that edge and they aren't doing anything for themselves. If you ask them the same question of what did they do when they got to that ledge, they will say the same thing: THEY JUMPED! There are two parts to this equation in this life experience. The first is whether or not you are willing to jump!! Are you a wisher, a watcher, or a maker? It takes a lot of confidence to even take that jump. The second part of the equation is the difference between the people that failed and the ones that became successful? They both jumped, so what is the difference? It is really simple. Some kept on believing in themselves and others did not. Doubt will prevent anyone from becoming successful when they are doing something.

As a former athlete, I know what it is like to have to

believe myself to be successful. I need that to transfer beyond the playing field to the real world. The playing field will change one day. The playing field will become the real world. That competitive drive will be there long after the game is over. The question is are you willing to jump? Are you willing to bet on yourself? Do you believe that you can be successful at something because you are doing it? Are you going to put the time and work into being successful? That is the exact same thing that we did when we were competing in sports. We believed in ourselves. We saw other teams that were being successful. We knew what they were doing, and we did it. We also saw others that were not being successful and saw what they did and did not do. This philosophy does not have to change in what we call the real world.

The principles that define us, push us, and make us are

there already! We just have to transfer them into something else, go about it the same way and get the same success.

> *"The principles that define us, push us, and make us are there already"*

Don't spend your life being a wisher or a watcher. Don't get me wrong we all have to be a wisher and a watcher at some point in time but the key to it is to stay in the first two categories as short as possible and exist in the realm of being a maker for as long as you can!

## Chapter 3
## The Decision Why: *what is the decision-making process and why is it so important?*

Have you ever heard the term "pain before pleasure"? There is a reason why that is said when you choose to take a path to success. There are going to be let-downs, there will be disappointments, there will be sacrifice, and there will be failure. What I have learned is that it is just a part of the burden you have to bear to be great and be at the top of your profession; whatever it is that you do. Pain, sacrifice, disappointment, let-down, failure, and flat out struggle is a part of success because that is what makes the difference between the ones that are successful and the ones that are not. I can assure you that all of it is a part of the recipe.

Embracing it is where the true transition from average to successful takes place. All of that revolves around 2 simple things. A decision and a decision-making process.

I think back to when I opened up the first business of my own, completely independent of any type of parent company for support. As I was building the business I had an interviewing process for hiring people. This one gentleman I interviewed, talked to me about his desire to succeed after the military and how it has been difficult for him to transition back into the civilian world. I hired him. I personally took him out and trained him. Every day he would come back to the office with a story behind why he was not successful. After a few days I went out to shadow him and see why he was getting the results he was getting. He was negative from start to finish. Negative about what he was doing, how he was doing it, and even the people we were talking to. I asked him why he kept coming back? He said because he believed in me and what I was doing. I decided to keep him on and give him another chance. Our client needed help in another market and agreed to foot the hotel room for a business trip into town. I decided to send him. I wanted to give him an opportunity to focus completely on work. I gave him a gas card and He drove down to the hotel and checked in. Within an hour he called me complaining about the quality of the hotel. I reminded him that the client booked the hotel and I had no control over that, but I would book him another one the next day. The gentleman quit that night and drove back up at 3 a.m. A week later I see a negative review of my company telling that exact same story from his perspective with an anonymous as the author. He never even spoke to me to clear the situation up but went on to write negative things about me and my company. That is an example of uncontrollable instances of disappointment. That was not the first time I faced disappointment and it definitely was not the last. Deciding to push beyond the many disappointments is one of the toughest things you can do. It has to be done.

We do understand what decisions are and we understand that our life's results are based on the decisions that we make. Understanding our decision-making process helps us understand why we come up with some of the decisions that we end up making. Regardless of what the situation is, we all have a process that we use to make our decisions. The better we understand it, the better the decisions we will be able to make. If I base my decision-making process off of solid core beliefs and principles that other models of success have, then I am sure to get similar results. This works very effectively when done consistently over the course of time. Great decisions are the foundation of great success. Great decisions are truly a reflection of a sound decision-making process.

*"Pain, sacrifice, disappointment, let-down, failure, and flat out struggle is a part of success because that is what makes the difference between the ones that are successful and the ones that are not"*

Here is an example of a decision-making process that I came across and I still find it to be remarkably effective. Mind you that I did not make this up; I am simply passing along knowledge that I have obtained.

<u>Decision vs. Outcome</u>

Wrong decision at wrong time = chaos

Wrong decision at the right time = mistake

Right decision at the wrong time = resistance

Right decision at the right time = success

# Chapter 4
# Self Image:

***The importance of Self-Image and how it relates to being successful***

Self-discovery, self-image, self-identity. These were things that I did not consider until my mentor addressed them with me. I only thought about them when I lost my own self-identity. I want to give you a clear definition of each, so we know what we are thinking about when we reference these perspectives in our own life.

- Self-discovery: the process of acquiring insight into one's own character.
- Self-identity: the recognition of one's potential and qualities as an individual especially In relation to context.
- Self- image: the idea one has of one's abilities, appearance, and personality.

When you lose your identity, you will lose your self image and then you will lose your self-confidence. If you have risen to the top at any point in your life and you have fallen from that point you will realize at some point in time that you are not where you used to be. That is when you really begin to question your identity, your image, and your confidence.

Let us take a look at how that happens. A lot of times we lose our self-identity when we begin to attach ourselves to something else. The more we attach ourselves to that thing the less we remain who we are. Before you know it we are not what we used to be and that is how we get lost. I know this to be true because I have done this before in my lifetime. I was once in a relationship that I put so much into that I lost my identity wanting to attach myself to that person and that relationship. Things do not work well that way at all. I lost more than I gained in that situation, but I did learn more about myself, so it was not a total loss. I learned a major lesson in life that I carry with me now. YOU ARE RESPONSIBLE FOR YOUR OWN HAPPINESS. Please understand that aspect of life. The sooner the better. There are tons of people out there that seem to have it all but if they do not find happiness within, there is nothing external that can provide it.

As far as self-image, it goes beyond what we look like externally. It also plays into how we feel internally. That is probably more important than any external factor. If we consistently believe that our image is not where it should be we are going to live life that way. We are going to live our lives not having the proper image we should have for ourselves. When we get lost like that the perception that we have of ourselves gets negative, it gets down, and it becomes low. When that time comes, do not expect anyone to perceive you differently than you perceive yourself. Self-image is important. It goes back to loving ourselves and appreciating ourselves. I remember listening to a conference call and the speaker was talking about image and being sharp when you present yourself. "How sharp you are has nothing to do with money but has everything to do with effort," he said. "You can go out and buy a $1000 suit and don't iron it or keep it clean and look less presentable than the person that got their suit from the goodwill that cleaned and ironed there's. That has nothing to do with how much something cost." If you love and appreciate everything you have you will perceive everything you have differently.

The last thing is your self-confidence. What will make

you lose confidence in yourself? It's amazing that it happens because we all should believe in ourselves, but sometimes we lose our confidence based off of things that happened to us, especially when things don't go the way we thought they would go or the way we hoped they would. I opened a marketing firm in Memphis, Tennessee in 2008. At the time I had three locations in operation. We had one of the fastest growing organizations in the company. Within a year all three companies closed, and I was out of business. I remember sitting at home after that failure and my mentor gave me a call. After listening to me for 5 minutes he told me to stop feeling sorry for myself. He said, "You are where you are because of you whether it's good or bad." If you are in a bad or good place in life you may have gotten help in getting there but you drove the vehicle. Three months later I opened another business and we grew 3 times the size of my business before. Self-confidence and self-discovery helped me regain my self-image and self-identity. When things do not go the way that we think they should, we lose confidence in our ability to believe in ourselves because things did not turn out the way you wanted them to. We all have a perfect image of things being the way we want them to be from beginning to end before we even start to do anything. When challenges come into play is when reality kicks in. Life is not about things going the way we want them to go. It is about adjusting to things when they happen. As a former athlete I can say that identity, image, and confidence played a huge factor into how far I went. To get to a certain level as an athlete you have to have all of that. We get to that level sometimes and after the game is over we lose our identity because we only identified ourselves as the type of athlete we were like football, basketball, track, etc. Your greatness as an athlete or anything else you may excel at is only a portion of the greatness you have in you as a person. Just identify who you are as a whole person and you will be fine.

Have you ever been with someone and you built a life with them then all of a sudden it falls apart? Lots of times people lose themselves in that situation. I have been a part of losing myself that way. I encourage you to do this. Always have an identity separate from your partner. That does not mean you should not grow with them, but it does mean that you should always have your own identity. If you lose them you do not want to lose yourself at the same time.

When you are forced to change into something else, that does not mean your core identity needs to go away. Being confident, being strong, and believing in yourself are things that you can carry with you no matter where you go or what you do.

> *"If you have risen to the top at any point in your life and you have fallen from that point you'll realize at some point in time that you're not where you used to be. That is when you really begin to question your identity, your image, and your confidence"*

# CHAPTER 5

# Failing vs. Quitting:

*There is a difference between the two and how they relate to success*

Losing is not the opposite of success, quitting is. That is what determines if a person is successful or unsuccessful. It is not whether you fail it is whether or not you quit. I think about back to playing and coaching sports and participating in competitive drills. At times, a person may fall down while doing that drill. Coach would tell them to get up and finish. Even if they had lost the contest the coach would tell them to get up and finish strong. Why? Because you are not a quitter if you finish. That is what will determine if you are going to be successful in the long run.

My third-year coaching HS football I was at West Ashley High in Charleston SC. There was a big kid walking around the school who had never played before. Of course, you know the coaches stayed after the kid until he decided to come out and play. I mean this kid was a massive 6'6" 320lb kid. Yet, he could not play a lick of football! He played that year and decided to come back for his senior year. After an unproductive high school career, he decided that he wanted to play in college, so he went to a junior college in Kentucky. He stayed there for a year and when his mother got sick he came home and finished up at a technical school. His desire to play college ball was still there. The following year he enrolled at the University of South Carolina and tried out for football. He got cut. Worked out and came back out and tried out again. He got cut again. By this time most anybody would have given up on that dream and moved on. Not him. He tried out again. Third time was a charm! He made the team! He was officially a practice dummy. Well, that was not enough for him. As the season began he stole every rep he could with the 2nd and 3rd team and even the scout team so he could get better. Remember that "last Man standing" quote from earlier? Well that was him. While injuries came and others were inconsistent he stayed steady and confident in his work ethic and became a starter. He went on to become an all SEC player and signed a free agent deal with an NFL team. There are more twists and turns to this young man's journey, but I can assure you that even what you learned today is more than what most could bare. He never quit in the face of adversity.

I know many people have seen the commercial before with Dwyane Wade falling down a lot when he won his first title back in '06. The caption at the bottom of the screen said fall down seven times and get back up eight. That's why he is a champion. He could take those falls knowing he was going to hit the ground and knowing he was going to get back up continuing to fight. That is what it's all about. I cannot count how many times I've failed in my life. I don't even want to count. The only time that I wasn't a success in my life is when I gave up on what I was doing. I am an example of someone who has given up on something in life and lost because of it. In my last year of college, I had an opportunity to transfer after the head coach had dismissed me from the team. I was so hurt and so angry that I pushed my dreams of playing at the next level to the back of my mind. I gave up on them. By the time that window of opportunity had closed there was no going back to it. I had to live with my decision. The loss of that opportunity is what motivated me so much with the next opportunity. That moment played a major role in me becoming who I am now. If I told you that I never gave up in my life, I would be telling you a lie. But what I can say is when I've given up, I've lost more than just what I had at that time. Sometimes you just can't get that back. That's called losing opportunity. Transition is not the time to give in or give up. Think about what you were before your transition began to happen. How dedicated you were to what you were doing? How hard did you work to separate yourself from others that did the same thing that you did? Did something change about you? The answer is no. The only way that you won't be successful at doing something else, other than what you were characterized or defined as before your transition, is quitting on yourself.

> *"Always remember failure is a part of success.*
> 
> *Losing isn't failure. Quitting is"*

In chapter 3 The Decision and Why and in chapter 4 Self Image I spoke briefly about when I opened my company in North Carolina. I talked a little about how it started and scenarios that occurred in the early days. What I didn't talk about was how it got off the ground. I had no capital to start that business. Heck I didn't even have a sales force. I went into the meeting with my client with me being the only person in my company. They believed in me and my vision enough to give me a shot. I pieced together a few guys from some companies that had failed before in the markets I was set to enter. I had no money to provide a payroll. I took out a $5000 title loan on a car that my mother had just paid for. We didn't even have an office space to work out of. I got up and printed leads out of the local library every morning. When I was able to pull together my first team I had 2 guys from one office that failed and 3 more guys from another office that had failed in another market. I had one other guy that came with me to start with. A few of the guys stayed in a hotel my client had provided for them and I stayed with my cousin on his floor in Durham NC. I called the group of guys together and told them that we got paid once a month and I had no money for payroll the first month. I told them that if they didn't quit and believed in the vision I would take what I had (from the title loan) and help them pay their bills for that first month. They bought in. That following month I was able to put checks of no less than $5000 in each of their hands! What a wonderful feeling that was! Here it is a group of guys that all came from companies that failed. We were all in some of the toughest situations you could imagine but we didn't quit. Trust me there is a difference between failing and quitting.

# CHAPTER 6
# Winning and Influencing People:

*A process of how to win people over by getting them involved and celebrating their success*

Have you ever heard the term; strength comes in numbers? It's true. I want to give you an example of how strength in numbers works. Influence goes in direct correlation with growing numbers.

In July of 2005 I moved to Charlotte NC to take a job in a sales and marketing firm. I moved there with nothing. I went to stay with one of my fraternity brothers from school who had moved there a few years earlier. When I got to his home, I was impressed to say the least! I mean this was the same guy from college that was hanging out and being one of the lives of the party. He somehow transformed that into who I met when I came to see him. I remember asking him this question: "How did you go from that to this?" He then shared that there came a point in time in life where he had to put everything down and focus on himself. All of the friends, family or females weren't going to get him where he needed to be. "I had to do it myself." That is what he said to me. A great piece of wisdom for someone in my position to hear at that time. Most definitely played an influential part in my grasping of reality. Well the story didn't end there. Not even a week into being there one of his family members had some trouble back home and needed to relocate, so I had to go.

Due to the sensitivity of the situation it was best for all parties. I was out in the city of Charlotte doing door to door sales in the day and I slept in my 1996 Chevy Tahoe at night. Fortunately, one of the guys that was on the same crew as me, saw my situation and wanted to give me some help by offering me a place to sleep. Once again I had been helped by someone else. Those are just a few of the things that led up to me building the type of business that I built. My company motto was "people helping other people". Experiences like those and many more are what led me to have a desire to see other people win as a result of their own efforts while I just help them along the way. In order to win and influence people you must have a server's mentality first. What can I do to help you? Once people know you are simply there to help them, these five steps will play a key role in influencing them.

There are five steps to winning influence with others.

**Step one:** is to create a vision. That vision must be large enough to include not only you, but others who play a part in making the vision happen. The vision has to be larger than life itself. There was a Roman leader named Marcus Aurelius who said, "Dream big dreams, because only the big dreams have the power to move men's souls." When you have created a vision and you want to win and influence others; that vision must be large enough for others to see themselves in it. Bill Gates is a great example of this. He created a vision larger than life right out of his own garage! Here is a person that had a vision of changing the world around him. He believed in his vision so much that he dropped out of school and began chasing his vision full time out of his garage. When you speak of courage and having a big vision you can look at Gates as an example.

**Step two:** in winning influence with others is to show others how you are going to get to that vision that you have created. There is nothing that people respect more than an example for them to follow when it comes to patterning success. When there is a model of success that people can follow they are a lot more on board for jumping in and getting involved in making that vision happen and becoming successful. Kobe Bryant was a great example of how an individual embodied being the example. I'm gonna get it done regardless of any situations or circumstances is what the "**Mamba Mentality**" is all about! Before he left us tragically in 2020, he had already retired from a hall of fame career and was on the way to becoming a business Mogul. He was involved in a venture capitalist business that he and his partner grew from a $100 million to a $2 billion dollar business portfolio in just a few short years.

He was the leader and the example and that gave others comfort and confidence in following.

*"There is nothing that people respect more than an example for them to follow when it comes to patterning success"*

**Step three:** is to show people how they play a part in a vision of success. Most people want to be a part of something bigger than themselves. Sooner or later most people want to be responsible for something bigger than themselves as well. In order to become responsible and effectively play a part in a vision you must learn and accept being a part of something bigger than yourself at first. If you want to win over others you must be willing to give them something to be a part of. Once people want to be a part of the vision you have created, you find what their goals are and how they are attached to your vision. When I first started in sales they used to have a process at night that highlighted successful performances of the day. It was called ringing the bell. When you hit $100 plus dollars in production for the day you could go up and ring the bell in front of everybody. Not everyone rang the bell every day. Not everyone did but the crew I was on did. All the people that were on the same team as I, were producing every day. I wanted in! I wanted to be a part of that! I did! Before you know it, I was a high roller. Wasn't long before the itch hit me again. I didn't want to just be productive myself. I wanted to be responsible for teaching others as well. The rest is history!

**Step four:** naturally comes from step three. Once you have identified with their purpose and reason for being a part of your vision, you as a leader must put their purpose or their goals in front of yours! Whatever it is that they have attached to your vision, it becomes your responsibility to push them to be successful in it. This creates the ultimate buy-in. When you are willing to put yourself last for the betterment of someone else they will always want to be a part of what you have going on. My best friend joined the military as a commissioned officer after doing college ROTC for 4 years. Not sure if you know how it works but I will educate you if you don't. Commissioned officers come in and have instant rank over lots of people in the military that may have tons more of actual military experience. This can sometimes cause a rift in the command structure when an officer comes in and doesn't respect their soldiers. My best friend knew that and refused to use his position to command respect. He earned it. He told me a story about how he was leading a convoy and one of the tires had blown out on one of the vehicles. The first thing he did was jump off of his vehicle and run to the lead vehicle and he got down and started changing the tire himself without asking anyone to help. He Said he wasn't going to order someone to do something that he was capable of doing himself. He gained the respect of his entire unit that day. Always remember that people want to be a part of and eventually be responsible for something bigger than they are. Find a way to accommodate both of those scenarios and you will always be able to win in influencing others.

**Step five:** is the final part to influencing others. It revolves around expectations. The expectations fall on the people that you have helped. Once you have been an example to others in how to create a vision, show people how you are going to get there, show them how they play a part, and put their goals in front of yours. You then set expectations for them to do the same thing for others that you have done for them. Major changes happen in people's lives once they accept that responsibility. Not only do they change or enhance their situation they more than likely improve the situations of many others that follow their example. This process leads to explosive growth! Find a way to incorporate this scenario of developmental tactics in your process and you will always be able to win in influencing others.

*"Dream big dreams, because only the big dreams have the power to move men's souls" - Marcus Arelious*

Always remember that people want to be a part of and be responsible for something bigger than they are.

# CHAPTER 7
# Think Big, Act Big, Get Big:
*Success starts in the mind and plays out in the real world. How does that process work?*

I will be the first to say that this thought is not original. It is not the first time that these words have been spoken, written, or grouped together and it won't be the last. What I will say about this quote is that it is a reality for those living it start to finish. Everything starts in a place where dreams can become reality. It starts off in the mind.

Do you know who Emmitt Smith is? I do! Hall of fame NFL all-time leading rusher. Yep that's him. Well before all that happened he was a kid playing college ball at the University of Florida. When he got drafted he was interviewed by some reporters. One of the reporters asked him what his goal was now after being drafted into the league. The young Emmitt Smith who had never played an NFL down said that he wanted to break Walter Peyton's record as the all-time leading rusher. Smith wasn't the fastest strongest or quickest back in the league by far. One reporter said well how do you plan on doing that? Emmitt replied saying "by outworking everyone else." He said if he could be consistent and keep playing he might have a chance. Well in a game in 2002 against the Seahawks Smith became the all-time leading rusher passing the great Walter Peyton. Think Big Act Big Get Big!

How many times have you listened to someone else's idea or had a great one of your own in your head? Everything makes so much sense there. The idea may not be totally planned out but the distance between the thought of the idea and the actual reality of that idea coming to life seems so short. "Think of it today and it is here tomorrow" seems easy right? Then reality kicks in. Something is missing. Why aren't my ideas and dreams becoming a reality?

Well I missed one major part of the equation: ACTION! You have to have that action if you really want to make something happen! No one is going to do it for you. We have to take personal responsibility and get it done for ourselves. After all, the idea is just an idea until you physically go through the process of making it a reality. If you have a great idea and you share it with someone else and then take no action to make it become reality, don't be surprised or upset if that person acts and makes your dream become their reality. After they have taken the action to make it become a reality, whose dream is it then? You can't just think your dreams into existence. You have to live them out. That is how the process works. That is the bridge between a dream and a reality. This book is a perfect example of it. I've thought of writing this book for the last seven years of my life. I've expressed the idea to friends and colleagues. I have even gone as far as looking up editors and speaking to publishing companies. All that sounds good but until I put this pen to this paper it was all a dream. If you have this book in your hand right now, or you are reading it on a screen or listening to it you are actually witnessing a dream come true. Action is what makes a dream become a reality.

> *"You can't just think your dreams into existence.*
> 
> *You have to live them out"*

# CHAPTER 8
# Don't Work Me Hard:
### *How does hard work relate to success?*

In the fall of 1999, I transferred schools to continue my career as a collegiate athlete at the University of South Carolina. I had always dreamt of playing major college football and competing against some of the best players in the country. I finally had the opportunity to make my dream come true. Once again I found my destiny in my own hands.

Before being able to practice we had tryouts to see if we could make the team as a walk-on. This isn't a little league or high school tryouts. You actually will get cut if you don't show the skill level that they are looking for to help the team win. I made the team within 30 minutes of the try-out.

This part of my story is not about me, making the team, or about the many teammates that went on to play at the next level. This story is about something that everyone on the team and many other teams heard if they played for Lou Holtz. This was Lou Holtz's first year at USC and we had just come off of a 1-10 season the year before. To make things worse we went 0-11 that season. We simply did not have the mentality or the athletes we needed to be competitive at that time. It was more a lack of mentality than it was a lack of talent though.

The mentality of losing settled in and that's what had to change to move forward. I can remember the first day out at practice. We were stretching beforehand. As I was sitting in my stretch line I saw a frail or older man riding up to practice on a golf cart. As he began to walk towards me I began to smell the scent of the cigar that he seemed to have with him at all times. As he got closer I began to get nervous. I had never been around a football personality of that magnitude. I mean, this was Lou Holtz! He had won a national title and coached many NFL greats like my favorite player growing up, Jerome Bettis!

Just as I thought he was going to walk past me, he stopped right beside me and said, "Lewis."

I surprisingly looked up and said, "Yes sir?"

Coach Holtz replied with, "I heard about you. Keep up

the good work. I want to see what you got."

I was thinking to myself, how? We haven't even practiced yet. He began to walk down the lines and make comments to other players while we were stretching, and that's when he said it.

He said, "Hey guys! If you don't feel like working hard just look at me and say, 'I don't want to be great' and I'll leave you alone!"

He repeated that statement again and again before eventually blowing the whistle and beginning practice. That quote has forever been etched into my mind. *"Don't work me hard, I don't want to be great!"*

It is one of the simplest yet one of the most motivating statements I have ever heard in my life. I went hard every day naturally but on days I was not 'feeling it' for some reason I would always revisit that quote in my mind. As a coach I continue that tradition with all the players that I have coached. I can assure you that every one of them can attest to that statement because that is a quote they probably heard at least 5 to 10 times a week from me throughout their entire football playing career under me. "If you don't feel like doing it just look at me and say, 'Don't work me hard coach, I don't want to be great." I quickly learned that this statement is not only true in sports. It relates to business and life.

After the game was over and the helmet and shoulder pads came off for the last time I continued to allow that quote to live in me and live through me. It applies to anything that we do. Hard work is a key to success. Hard work separated winners from losers. The following year we had the biggest turnaround in NCAA football history going from 0-11 to 8-4 and had a win in the Outback Bowl against a powerful Ohio State team. Just goes to show you the power of words and actions once they are internalized and lived.

*Hard work is a key to success. Hard work separated winners from losers.*

# CHAPTER 9
# Momentum and Motivation:

*How momentum leads to motivation and motivation leads to success*

What do you do when you get off track and stay off track? What is the next step? I can tell you from experience being a person that has been on track, stayed on track when things have gone my way, and stayed off track when things haven't gone my way.

In the summer of 2012, my sales offices were mediocre at best. I was physically and emotionally drained. One week I was in my hometown and I went to visit my old high school. They were having practice in the gym. I watched those kids run around for about an hour. I got close enough to the kids to ask them their names and who their parents were. To no surprise many of the kids were children of my classmates or people I went to school with. I fell in love. I showed up that afternoon and I kept showing up for the next 5 years! I became a coach and eventually a coordinator. This experience in my life provided the energy source I needed to recharge from the draining that came from my previous career. Before 2012 we had not made the playoffs since 2002 and had three 0-10 seasons while having only 1 player go to the next level. That all changed over the next 5 years. In that time, we had 5 consecutive years of making the playoffs. Not only did we make the playoffs in that time we had a run to the lower state championship game. My first graduating class won more games in a 4-year span than any other graduating class in school history. That was merely the icing on the cake. The biggest thing to happen was the 14 kids that signed national letters of intent to pursue their dreams of being a collegiate athlete. I was motivated! I was motivated to have an opportunity to affect change in a community that so desperately needed it. The passion that came out of me and it was contagious. That motivation led to momentum which helped to spark one of the most powerful feelings of accomplishments in my life. You have to figure out how to get momentum and keep that momentum going. Once you get to the place where you have figured out a way to keep the momentum going, you will stay on track. You have to identify what your motivating factors are. My motivating factor in that part of my life was seeing positive change in the youth of my community. Most people that have traveled a path similar to mine with a sports background would say that the motivating factor is being successful. What I have found is that people who may not have had a sports background but have been a part of the daily process of making it happen are motivated by the same things the same way. That motivation is success as well. So then comes the deeper question. What determines an individual's success?

There is a broad answer to that question. What isn't broad is the fact that through all of those things that may bring the type of success a person wants to have in their life, the common denominator is that all of them are going to take work to get there.

How does motivation play a part in success? What is motivation? "Motivation is a person's reasons for acting or behaving in a particular way." Success has a pattern. If your motivation causes you to act in a particular way that is productive and moving toward your goals of success then you are on the right track. Interestingly enough, momentum is defined as a strength gained by motion or by a series of events. When motivation can get you going in the right direction, momentum will most definitely take you to that destination called success.

*"At the end of the day, it's all about what you want and desire. That's what's going to make things happen."*

I moved to Kansas City, KS in September of 2006 to open my first business. Moved 18 ½ hrs. away from home into a house with 6 people that I had known no more than a year at the most. These people followed me to help me pursue my dreams while I helped them pursue theirs. The first 4 months were pretty tough. I was barely making payroll on the business side. On the personal side I had 6 people away from home in an environment that was completely new. Not to mention the cold! I had never been so cold in my life! We were very slowly moving along until I interviewed an 18-year-old kid from the streets of Kansas City and decided to hire him into my company. He changed everything. This kid was hungry! I mean hungry! He told me if I could show him how to make money any other way than what he was doing he was all in! Well I showed him, and the rest is history. He transformed the mentality in my office. He eliminated all the excuses the older guys were making and started bringing results. Shortly after he brought a few of his friends to work in his newfound profession. Before long we had risen to the top spot as the #1 vendor in the country. It's amazing how one person's motivation led to a company's resurgence of momentum. Sometimes all you need is one. How often is that one you?

# CHAPTER 10

# Being Extraordinary:

*What is the difference between ordinary and extraordinary?*

Do you know what accepting the responsibility of greatness means? It means that if you don't reach your full potential in life you give someone else a reason not to reach theirs. In saying that you also have to consider that someone is always watching your actions. Someone is always watching or hearing about something you do. No one is perfect by any means. No one always does all the right things all the time. What makes a person extraordinary is doing the right things at the right time. That's what allows the separation of ordinary and extraordinary.

I was watching a documentary the other day about a

football team, its coach, and his philosophy on the position that he coached. He told the players what would make them successful. What he told the players was he could teach them all the technical and fundamental aspects of the game that they needed to know and put them in a position to be successful, but at the end of the day it's going to be all about their want and desire that's going to make things happen. He was right.

I went to a Tony Robbins convention and listened to the motivational speaker and author talk about the ingredients you must have to be an extraordinary person and have an extraordinary life. The main ingredient was hunger. I look back to when I was moving through the business model that helped me become successful and I would talk about three core things that were involved.

One thing for sure is that you have to constantly develop your skill set. Whatever your strong point is, be sure to get it stronger by constant development. You have to have a burning desire to be successful. A burning desire separates you from everyone else. That's the biggest difference in having an ordinary or an extraordinary life in this world. The other special ingredient is work ethic. This book has talked about all three of those things in some shape, form, or fashion. Find those things in yourself and you will find yourself being successful.

Kanye West made a song called "Good Morning". In that song is one of my favorite quotes. He says: *"on this day we become legendary; everything we dreamed of"*. I just love that part of that song because it makes me think about the fact that there is a journey that we must take before we get to any destination. When you dream of something that hasn't happened yet, it means that it's still in your mind. When you say 'on this day you become legendary' you are saying that today marks the day that my dream will become a reality. Ordinary people have dreams, but extraordinary people turn those dreams into realities.

> *"Ordinary people have dreams, but extraordinary people turn those dreams into realities"*

# ABOUT THE AUTHOR

Travis Lewis is a multifaceted creative, business owner and author. He currently resides in Charleston, SC where he continues to educate people about the importance of finding their niche and creating a solid plan to turn it into a business.

A native of Latta, SC originally, Travis was a 3 sport athlete at Latta High School. He received an athletic scholarship to attend ETSU in Johnson City, TN. After 2 years with the Bucs, he decided he wanted to chase his dreams of playing at the division 1 level. He left his full scholarship for an opportunity to walk on at the University of South Carolina. Now having to pay tuition, Travis took out student loans and began working as a server at a local

Applebee's. Going to class and working everyday he still found time to attend every practice, meeting, and work out while posting the highest GPA of his college career. In that semester he managed to earn a full athletic scholarship and convert to fullback and letter the following year for a team that had the biggest turn around in NCAA history. Everything seemed to be going as planned. Travis was living his dream. The spring of 2001 changed everything.

www.ingramcontent.com/pod-product-compliance
Lightning Source LLC
Chambersburg PA
CBHW020958090426
42736CB00010B/1379